The Dance of
Herodias Daughter

The Dance of Herodias Daughter

Revealing Satan's Last Deception in the Church

God'spower E O Udjor

authorHOUSE®

AuthorHouse™
1663 Liberty Drive
Bloomington, IN 47403
www.authorhouse.com
Phone: 1-800-839-8640

First published by AuthorHouse   11/21/2011

ISBN: 978-1-4567-8158-3 (sc)
ISBN: 978-1-4678-7820-3 (ebk)

All scriptures quotations are from the King James Version of the Bible except otherwise stated.

Printed in the United States of America

Contents

ACKNOWLEDGMENTS

I want to thank God Almighty for letting me be the vessel to bring forth this book.

I am also very grateful to the pastor of our Kaduna church (Pastor Blessing Ogbonnah) for typing out the manuscript. Am thankful to God for bringing in Pastor Mrs. Puna Maiyaki, whose input has helped this book to become a reality. I'm grateful to God also for the great church workers He has given to me in our Abuja church.

I praise God for the life of Rev. & Rev Mrs Yinka Yusuf, Rev & Rev Mrs Mosy Madugba, and other great servants of God who believes in the restoration of God's Church.
I appreciate my lovely wife, Rev Mrs. Lydia U. Udjor who believes in the Grace of God on my life.

DEDICATION

To all those who DESIRE to see a RESTORATION in the Body of Christ.

Oh great Book . . . go into the world and by the Spirit of God do what the Lord has ordained you for.

Oh great Book . . . go into the world and be used of God to bring His Church back to Him.

INTRODUCTION

The spiritual climate has been greatly altered, that any sensitive person could easily discern the change. The release of demonic influence is so enormous that its thickness can be felt through the length and breadth of God's creation.

The manifestation of this influence is such that, at a glance, a spiritually minded individual can see it. All this unleashing of Hell's resources has been, however, permitted by God; for no Being can do anything without the express permission of the Almighty. God's purpose is always to establish our supremacy over Satan.

Hell and its heads have launched an all-offensive attack on the earth, narrowing it to the Body of Christ. These attacks come in several ways; the sole reason of this is to exterminate the Church and to wipe her off existence. The scheme of Satan is to destroy the Church, to make non-sense the work of Christ and gradually destroy the purpose of God. This evidently cannot be possible because through history, Satan had put-up desires and action like these. In trying to kill Moses and Jesus, he sponsored the destruction and killings of all the male children born at that time, totally annihilating innocent kids. God, however in His ultimate and infinite wisdom always has a way planned for the deliverance of His chosen.

<u>In the same vein, there is an on slaught on the church and the devil in using seeming Christians to thwart the work of God, thus creating maximum confusion among unbelievers and creating commotions within the church, because the bottom line is that our enemies are wearing our uniform.</u>

Satan knows that his time is short; he is therefore using every resource available in his arsenal against the church. He has and is applying the very temptation he gave to Jesus Christ Himself. For no temptation is higher than that which Jesus received. {1} that of man's stomach (turning stones to bread) {2} directly tempting God by twisting the scriptures and {3} by offering wealth and fame.

These are the highest weapons in Satan's armory and thus has he unleashed against the Church and unsuspecting minds.

There is something about John the Baptist. He was not just a man, he was a prophetic figure. He had prophecy hanging on him before birth. He has prophecy hanging on him after death. Understanding this unique figure of whom Jesus said *'of those born of a woman, none has*

ARISEN like John the Baptist", will give us a prophetic insight into satanic scheming; Satan hated John the Baptist.

The greatness or the RISE of John the Baptist was not connected to his descent or parental background but in his Calling and Purpose. It was his heralding of the coming Messiah that gave him his unique place in the graph of God. His significance was not in his ancestral lineage but on his assignment.

Just as Jesus Christ came before, and His coming was heralded by John, He is coming again, and His coming is being heralded again by John . . . for No ONE ELSE must herald His coming . . . . whether first or second Coming, except JOHN.

Silencing John was one of Satan's greatest priorities, because John's message had a great role to play in the manifestation of the Messiah. Just as salvation is not possible with repentance so is the relevance of John's message to Jesus message. Both lives were eternally connected.

AUTHOR'S NOTE

In 1st Kings 17, Elijah was introduced into the college of prophets in the Old Testament. His name which meant Yahweh is God was somewhat surprising as we never saw anyone bearing that name before his advent. He showed up in an era when Israel had strayed from God, giving heed to Baal and celebrating false prophets under the able sponsorship of Ahab and Jezebel.

Jezebel had either seduced or slaughtered all the true Prophets of Yahweh...and forced over seven thousand others into hiding. The shame and fear of standing alone was so strong that they hid themselves, however were still fed by Obadiah the king's servant.

This looks like the true picture of the today Church, which had come strangely under the influence of Jezebel...where falsehood is celebrated and applauded and the Truth has been driven to the backside of desert, into the obscure place of silence.

Just like God was painfully quiet when Jezebel slaughtered His prophets to the applause of falsehood, He has kept quiet over the grave state of His Church, watching Truth being slain in the altar of falsehood and drowned in the deceitfulness of riches, fame, fortune and congregational crowd.

Many have wondered at the silence of GOD and have mistaken it for His approval for falsehood; they have said **"why won't God just show up to stop this fellow if he is truly a false Prophet"?** This insensitivity to God's Person and Plan has increased the number of people plunging into falsehood in the **"if you can't beat them, join them syndrome"**, thus every preacher wants to become a **"Prophet"** of some sort.

Popularity at **"all cost"** is now the **"in thing",** consciously pushing aside the discipline of the Christian faith and celebrating compromise in its highest form as long as money and fame is attached.

Many have been initiated and have their soul sold to Satan already for the sake of church success. The irony is to think that one can be involved in the usage of Satan's power to do God's work. Folks have refused to understand **"that power belongs to God"** and they have also brushed aside the words of Jesus that **"a man's life does not consist of the abundance of things that he has"**...so POWER and wealth is being gotten from the devil and used in the pretence of service to God.

God had no Voice in the land. Falsehood dominated everywhere. Fear and irrelevance flanked the side of Truth, plunging it deeper into oblivion and obscurity. Gay Churches and the likes are springing up and surprisingly gaining overwhelming supports. All kind of falsehood is showing up in their magnitudes. Connection to high government officials and politicians are seen as major breakthroughs by Church leaders, which has invariably heightened the enormity of compromise and dumb the tongue of the Gospel.

Then suddenly from the wilderness of Tishbite came Elijah, with a Divine Mandate ...he hadn't been to any special Bible college, he had studied the protocol of talking to presidents to retain their favour, he doesn't understand the need to use cautious words in order to be invited back to the State House... he just appeared before Ahab and said **"as the Lord lives"...**

His duty was to announce that the Lord lives...and God equipped him with enough power to prove that indeed the Lord lives...

In the same vein, there are some whom the Lord is bringing in from every work of life...they will be seen as rebels...they won't run on titles but they will carry GOD in His fullness. Like Micaiah of old, they don't mind collecting slaps from spiritual fathers like Zedekiah (1st kings 22:6-24) but their words will never fall to the ground. They are the Voice of God in the wilderness, PREPARING THE WAY of the Lord for His Coming and which will give the midnight cry... CHURCH AWAKE, BEHOLD THE BRIDEGROOM COMETH.

CHAPTER ONE

WHO WAS JOHN?

The first prophecy of John is found in Isaiah 40:3. And this describes the real personality of John. John and Jesus shared the same origin. They both proceeded from God, but had different messages and purposes. John, at some point admitted that he didn't know Jesus, but He that sent him gave him a sign to look out for. "***I would not have known him, except that the One who sent me to baptize with water told me, 'the man on whom you see the Spirit come down and remain is He' I have seen and I testify that this is the Son of God"*** *John 1:33-34 (NIV)*

John according to Isaiah 40:3, was described as "The Voice..."in John's gospel chapter 1:14 Jesus was described as "The Word..." Both of them are representatives as they were not end in themselves. A voice ... of who? It said of "***One crying in the wilderness"*** John was not that person. He was the voice of that person. Jesus was the Word ... of whom? He was the word of God. John was the voice of God . . . a voice is a sound, an utterance but a word is a voice with meaning. A word is a voice constructed to give meaning.

John was not an ordinary being. He carried an anointing that stood him out. In Malachi's description of him, he was called "Elijah" (Malachi 4:5-6), in fact his prophecy was used to conclude the old testament, the very last words of the old testament.

In calling him Elijah, Malachi was referring to his mysterious nature . . . Elijah being a man without descent who came from NO WHERE, appeared before Ahab, announcing the reality of Jehovah. Elijah had no reference point. You cannot destroy him, because any permanent destruction must be done at the root, God concealed Elijah's root to make him indestructible. So God said, John is Elijah. When Jesus was to describe John, he got dramatic . . .

"what went ye out into the wilderness to see, A reed shaken with the wind?
"But what went ye out for to see? A man clothed in soft raiment? Behold, they which are gorgeously apparalled, and like live delicately are in Kings' court"
"But what went ye out for to see? A prophet? Yes I say unto you, much more than a prophet"
THIS IS HE, of whom it is written, Behold, I send my messenger (aggelos—ANGEL) before thy face which shall prepare thy way before thee . . . Luke 7:24-27

Another uniqueness of the tie between Jesus Christ and John, was Gabriel. This Arch angel had only four official appearances in the scriptures. The very first was when the Lord send him to explain a vision to Daniel, the second was when he came to give Daniel skill and understanding, the third and fourth time had to do with John and Jesus birth respectively.

The vision of Daniel and the birth of the twain was all inter-twined. But we shall leave that for another treatise.

As said in a sentence before, John wasn't the One talking in the wilderness . . . he was the "Voice" of the One. The difference between John and Jesus is the infallible fact that Jesus Christ is God . . . but John was a messenger. John however wasn't like the Voice of the prophets, they were all messengers, but John was the Voice of the Unseen Jesus, the Lord was heralding His own coming in the person of John. The spiritual utterance of Gabriel to both Elizabeth and Mary was directed to plant "Repentance" in Elizabeth and plant "Salvation" in Mary to the end that both are eternally united, for they were from One source.

The New Testament Call of God is to position every minister of the gospel on the platform of John. Not on a "covenant" or "locational" premise, but on bases of same message. John was an "Old Covenant" minister (in fact Jesus was also an Old covenant Minister, the New Minister only began when Jesus resurrected) and locationally, John, is below even the least in the kingdom of heaven(*Matt 11:11*).

Covenant and location wise, the New Testament Minister is higher than John. But the Purpose and Calling are one and same.

Whether the Calling is that of an Apostle, Prophet, Evangelist etc, the original purpose is to "perfect the saints" and getting them ready for the Messianic Arrival".

Isaiah said that through John's ministry ". . . ***every valley shall be exalted and every mountain and hill shall be made low, and the uneven shall be made level and rough places a plain . . . Isaiah 40:4 ASV***

John's ministry was to level all things. Nothing will be higher and nothing will be lower. The disciples will share all things in common—NONE will lack, there will be no rich and no poor. Yes Jesus said **. . . *"The poor you have with you always . . . (Mark 14:7),*** that scripture refers to those "outside" the Ark; for within the Ark of Noah, which was a type of a New Creation, none had too much and none lacked. Every mountain was low, and valley was lifted. This was John's ministry, for the Lord won't come if that balance was absent.

Malachi's said, John was to ***"turn the hearts of the fathers to the children and the hearts of the children to their***

fathers . . . God said if John does not succeed in this, He (God) will come and smith the earth with a curse..."Malachi 4:6 This is the ministry of the New Testament Ministry . . . the sum total of John's Ministry in New testament terms is ***"perfecting the saints" . . . Ephesians 4:12-13.***

But as always, John is the target of the devil. To detach him from his Call in every, and ANY way possible, even if it means beheading.

CHAPTER TWO

A MAN SENT FROM GOD

". . . there was a man sent FROM God, whose name was John" John 1:6. John was sent from God, not by God . . . To be "sent from" meant that he was with God. It was only on that ground that he could be a witness.

Legally, a witness is one who was either at the place of the event or has an evidence . . . John 1:7 said. *John the Baptist came as a witness*."

It is easy for those sent "by" God to derail, but hard for those "from" God to derail. Those from God are witnesses. That's why when the Holy Ghost comes, He makes us witnesses. We receive the Holy Ghost. Jesus received the Holy Spirit. Jesus received the Holy Spirit at baptism but we receive the Holy Ghost. The Spirit could only be called "Holy Ghost" after He left Jesus to enter into us; for a ghost is a spirit that has vacated a body.

He was in Jesus and made Him go through all He went through. The Holy Spirit made Him do all He did. So when He left Jesus, He became Holy Ghost and moved into the New Testament minister and made us witnesses. The person of the Holy Ghost in us is what classifies the minister as sent from God. There is, however, the issue of prophetic destiny . . . you can know more about that when you lay hold on my book—The Diary of God.

John the Baptist was "Sent"—APOSTELLO (Greek) . . . it means to be set apart properly on a Mission. His was specific. He is not permitted to derail. He was sent. The One that sent him gave him an assignment; to herald the coming of the Messiah.

As John was sent, so is EVERY SPIRIT-FILLED minister of the gospel, No matter what our Calling is, or no matter its varying nature, the Call is to prepare the way for the return of the Lord. God has no other reason of calling anyone if it's not for preparing the way.

Satan's target is aimed at those sent from God. He will do anything to kill a John the Baptist. As a minister of the gospel, not studying and identifying with John the Baptist's Call, is to live in perpetual ignorance. For every minister of the New Covenant, has no other Calling or reason for ministry other than this.

Apostle Paul said *". . . unlike so many, we do not peddle the word of God for profit. On the contrary, in Christ we speak before God with sincerity, like MEN SENT FROM GOD". II Cor. 2:17 (NIV)*

A sent man has a mission. A defined mission; His life is not hooked on vision. Many ministers are carrying and building visions. This has laid the foundation for the destruction of the church. In fact John's problem started when he started attending to vision.

Anytime there is a vision, a profit is sought for. Vision, unlike, as many people think, does not come from God, it comes from the mind of man. If vision comes from God, no unbeliever will have vision. Vision emanates from the mind of men where desires and ambitions meet.

The modern books on prosperity, great thinking and expansion of vision are not principally written by Christians. They are sponsored to magnify vision. Those sent "by" God entertains visions . . . those sent "from" God has a mission. Because before they escaped from eternity into time, their Call and Mission had been spelt out. For Jeremiah, God said *"before I formed thee in the belly, I knew thee, and before thou camest forth out of the womb I sanctified thee; I have APPOINTED thee a prophet unto the nations"—Jeremiah 1:5 (ASV).*

That is being "sent from" God. That was a mission. Not a vision of being a prophet to the whole world. Visions come from the mind. Visions are developed, but <u>PURPOSES ARE DISCOVERED.</u>

CHAPTER THREE

THE BIRTH OF A SENT MAN

Every man of God has a story connected to his birth and early childhood. Either documented or not, no anointed person has a regular conception, birth and early childhood. Something must happen along the line. Their lives suffer the threat of extinction in childhood. The devil studies their star and lunches early attacks. All sent people run on prophecy. They live pre-determined lives. Though some might stray through the acquisition of vision, the pre-determinate counsel of God has spelt out their mission and purpose. It will be either discovered or pursued or it will be swallowed by visions and ambitions. These are the constant battles between the mind (vision) and the Spirit (Mission).

As for John the Baptist, his entrance was through a barren couple. Sent people are a catalog of dramatic occurrences. From cradle to grave, sent people are constantly under attacks. They are on a mission and the opposition wants them out of the way at all cost. From Moses to the next anointed minister born this morning (that is still being breastfed), their lives are always dramatic. Every minister has a story to tell, otherwise how can he justify his being a witness?

When I read of the childhood of Archbishop Benson Idahosa of blessed memory, I saw all the traces of a "sent man". There are many ministerial figures and fathers today whose lives are a catalogue of stories about their childhood deliverance . . . they all have stories to tell.

Whatever you are going through is not tied to you. Your mission is what the devil is after. John the Baptist must be stopped ANYHOW. The inscription—wanted, dead or alive—was in Satan's notice board as soon as he was born. If you are a "sent" individual, your name has been there; since you were born.

Some people are however,—(because they are spiritually dead)-, no more a problem to Satan because, though, they were 'sent', they have however lost their Purpose and Mission. For them, Vision, which primarily deals with wealth, has swallowed purpose.

At his naming, a name that never existed in his family lineage was given to John, depicting a "New Creation" . . . . one that didn't exist in that family before. As a matter of Divine arrangement and structure, it's only New Creatures that can be Witnesses or Voices, heralding the return of the Master. Power and grace are made available to them.

John the Baptist was a man on a mission, deliberately living in the wilderness to avoid 'catching' a vision that would corrupt his purpose and mission; for when he moved into the city, his mission was compromised as we shall see.

A wilderness in this context is not a location. It is a state of mind. The "Voice" must cry in the wilderness because if the voice comes to town, it will be compromised. The city should go to him in the wilderness. The whole city came to John, he was practically insulting them, calling them vipers etc . . . yet they kept coming, because he was in the place where the "vision" was relevant—wilderness!.

Many "John the Baptist" (those called to herald the second coming) has left the wilderness which is the place of their relevance. So they have ceased to be a Voice, they are now ECHOES. An echo is the aftermath of a voice . . . Echoes are never originals . . . they are the diluted form of a voice, sometimes distorting the originals. When men become echoes, as we see around us in the Church, they just use the books and tapes of other people and the heavenly freshness of Divine Breath is forever lacking . . . and because the echo is masked in the deceit of charismatic displays, it easily passes as a voice in the ears of the already disillusioned populace. Especially in this era of rhymes and rhythmic preaching, the echo seems to scream louder than the voice . . . . The echoes however steadily fades away as it must be.

CHAPTER FOUR

THE MISSION

God announced that He would send His son to earth, and that a special Messenger would arrive first to PREPARE THE WORLD for His coming—Mark 1:2 (TLB).

The condition of the times before the coming of Jesus was such that God needed a John to do some preparations. Those were times when Israel got very religious. They connected to all forms of godliness. God in His wisdom had used Elijah to bring back the people to Himself before as in 1st Kings 18, so He sent John in the spirit of Elijah to set the stage for the coming Messiah. John's mission was clear. Prepare the world for His coming. No matter our congregational size, church structures, media vastness…the core purpose before the Messiah can come again is to prepare the world.

In Matthew 17:11-13, the Living Bible says, *"Jesus replied, 'they are right. Elijah must come and SET EVERYTHING IN ORDER. And in fact, he has already come, but he*

wasn't recognized and the disciples realized he was speaking of John the Baptist."

He was to put all things in order. And in him was the ability to do so. Why do you think "everyone" came to be baptized by John? God placed something in him and made his purpose to be noticed by all. He lived in the desert, yet everyone went to him, because he had a purpose. A man doesn't dream-up purpose or mission, you can dream-up a vision, you can construct a vision, you read a book and develop a vision, but, you CANNOT develop a MISSION or a PURPOSE. You can only DISCOVER A PURPOSE.

Purposes and Missions are things outside you. It's only one person that gives you purpose, only the MANUFACTURER. You can only look at the manual and discover the purpose.

You also don't create a mission. It must be someone other than you that sends you. That is why missionary have reference points, but visions and ambitions can originate from you and carried out by you.

Preparing the world, setting everything in order, perfecting the saints, bringing all things under Christ is our only reason for been Called of God.

John was to go before the face of the Lord, fore-running for Him to prepare His ways. Describing John the Baptist, the Apostle John said **. . . *"the same (John) came for A WITNESS, to BEAR witness of the Light, that men through John might believe . . . John 1:7.*** The word translated "a witness: (MARTURIA), means one armed with an evidence.

John's mission was clear—to make men aware of the coming messiah. That was his singleness of purpose. Satan hated John the Baptist, not for two or multiple reasons, but a SINGULAR reason . . . his being a WITNESS. A witness gives credence to a case. A witness validates a claim. So what the opponent fears more is the witness. Without a witness, the brilliancy or intelligence of the lawyer is irrelevant and off play. People do unimaginable things just to get rid of a witness. Satan didn't bother too much about Jesus, he bothered more about John. If there is no John, Jesus' claims would be irrelevant. So John is and has always been the target.

A witness with evidence is the greatest threat to an opponent. Every minister of the gospel is a 'MATURIA' that is, a witness armed with an evidence. And you are Satan's number one target.

It is amazing how we play with Satan and his toys when at the slightest opportunity, he would want us out of the way. Satan CANNOT STOP the gospel, but he wants to kill the witness.

A witness has only one job, to TESTIFY. John the Baptist was described as a witness. The NIV renders John 1:7 thus . . . *"He (John the Baptist) came as a witness to TESTIFY concerning the Light".*

CHAPTER FIVE

THE NAZARITE

Like every 'Way Maker', the voice in the wilderness must be a Nazarite or Nazarene. It is of utmost importance that every gospel minister should realize that they operate under a covenant. As a matter of spiritual experience, the witness and the one being witnessed for must be connected by a covenant. Thus John the Baptist was a Nazarene. However, the Nazarite covenant is one that operates within a time frame " . . . *he must operate within the ambit of the covenant . . . during the entire period . . . until the period of separation is over".* **Number 6:5.**

Though there are many laws to which the Nazarite must adhere, it is however worth noting that all come under the New Testament work of Jesus, summarizing all covenants in His blood. However, every witness must be connected to the Master. For as Jesus himself was the force behind John's witness, He too is our source for witnessing for Him, *as the branch cannot bear fruit without the vine,* **John 15:4**.

It amounts to spiritual fraud any attempt to testify for someone you scarcely know ... however, your relationship with the Master can greatly determine the credence of your testimony.

The witness is Satan's target ... In Matt 25, Jesus, being the ultimate wisdom of God, in whom culminates the entirety of all God is and has, puts up a strange parable wherewith He introduces a sect, whose appearance is of note . . . Though sandwiched silently in the passage, as they must need be, they are the greatest dread of the devil. Jesus talked about ten virgins . . . five were wise and five were foolish. Their level of wisdom was determined by their decision to get oil in their lamp . . . however, as beautiful as that story was, the Lord was teaching a deeper truth than "oil in lamps" . . .

He was rather introducing a sect of folks who were not among the virgins . . . they were neither wise nor foolish. They carried a different name and anointing . . . THEY WERE WITNESSES.

Satan was not bothered about the TEN VIRGIN (Mathew 25) . . . five that were wise and the other five that were foolish. They were not Satan's problem; *because he knew he could make all of them (wise or foolish) sleep.* What bothered Satan is the voice from the wilderness that will give the announcement. In Mathew 25:6 it says ' . . . ***and at midnight there was a CRY made, Behold, the***

bridegroom cometh . . . . ' These are the group that Satan is worried about. He worries about them because he can't get them to sleep, he worry because they operate at odd places (wilderness) and odd hour (midnight). Satan worries because these sects are not excited over what he has to offer. They prefer to live and minister in and from the wilderness; therefore, the temptation for wealth doesn't move them. They are satisfied with whatever God gives them. Locust and wild honey is just cool for them. They are ok with camel's hair for a garment. This, as noted earlier, are not literal but speaks of absolute dependence on God for food and clothing. After all the Master said, *". . . take no thought of the morrow . . . "* Satan does not know what to do with them.

These sects made their announcement at the odd hour . . . when Satan expected ALL to be sleeping . . . these guys prefer to be alive and alert at midnight, therefore the temptation for fame doesn't affect them. These are the John the Baptist Company. The enemy doesn't know what to do with them. Suffering doesn't bother them, enjoyment don't make them swell. Like the Apostle Paul, they know how to abound and to abase, they are WITNESSES. They must give the cry that the Bridegroom is coming. They are the voice in the wilderness; they give the cry at midnight. Their spiritual antenna is so high that they can pick Heaven's signals without straining themselves. Since they were expecting the Bridegroom anyway, like real armies in the war front, not entangling themselves with the affairs of this world, they created their own burn-fires waiting for the signals. As soon as they got it . . . they gave their cry . . . BEHOLD THE BRIDEGROOM COMETH . . . didn't that sound like REPENT FOR THE KINGDOM OF HEAVEN IS AT HAND? . . . scripture says John came baptizing in the WILDERNESS saying . . . repent for the kingdom of heaven is at hand.

Therefore the Lord Jesus Christ was introducing a sect of people instead of teaching on "oil and lamps" as our spiritual dullness could permit. The VIRGINS are the saints . . . those giving the CRY are the ministers . . . the witnesses who must do the job of PREPARING the Saints . . .

A Nazarite, who is a man on covenant, a man in the wilderness, and a man at midnight, is Satan's number one enemy. He is a major target; and serious problem because Satan is at lost as to what to use to tempt or destroy him. These are the people that can say *'your money perish with you'.* They can say *"leave your gift by (not on) the altar, go reconcile your heart first then come and offer your gift".* They are mission minded. They are purpose-guided. They are not vision driven and ambition minded. They are servants of God . . . they are witnesses.

5:1 FAILED MISSION
No man that warreth entangleth himself with the affairs of this life; that he may please him what hath chosen him to be a soldier. II Timothy 2:4

A soldier is a man with a mission. An avowed fighter of protection; A man with a mission has only one person to please . . . that is he, who sent him. Same is purpose; purpose pleases only one person, the manufacturer. Vision and ambitions however, pleases you, the carrier. As afore declared, a man can't send himself on mission, someone else does that and you are liable to that person.

In the case of John the Baptist, his job description was clear . . . he was the **'voice' crying in the wilderness '. . . preparing the way of the Lord.'** The Lord must come, so John's job was very relevant. Jesus is coming again, so our job is relevant. We and John share the same Calling, for there is no other!

John, however, failed. He became political . . . Herod became his ambition. He didn't see Herod in the wilderness. That would mean that John the Baptist came to town.

John was a force. Jesus said among those born of a woman, none has arisen like John . . . His greatness was in his Calling. As long as he stayed in the wilderness, within the perimeter of his Call, he had the ambiance of heaven. The wild beast of the jungle respected him. John's words were so strong that it pieced through men's heart, forcing their hearts to humble within them until entered the Jordan's river for baptism forgetting their personalities. The Scripture said "the whole city came to him".

John however, left his job of "crying in the wilderness and giving the midnight shout", to thinking that making impact with government was a great idea. Whether it was a rebuke or a praise, John the Baptist wasn't suppose to have a dealing with Herod, it was far from his Calling. It was a deviation and an aberration!

Jesus had said that John was not *"a reed shaken with the wind . . . neither was he supposed to have anything to do with the Palace"* (Matthew 11:7-8); Jesus said John was *"more than a prophet"* vs. 9, He was described thus because all of the prophets prophesied until John, he was the final voice, giving the announcement of the coming Messiah. The other prophets saw it from afar, but he was the voice of the hidden Christ, *"proceeding from Edom with dyed garment from Bozrah".* John the Baptist was the voice of him *'that is glorious in his apparel, travelling in the greatness of his strength . . . that speak in righteousness, mighty to save"* Isaiah 63:1

Satan has sought all means to destroy John; He could not until John wondered into the political terrain.

CHAPTER SIX

THE POLITICAL TERRAIN

John was John. Powerful, authoritative, feared and valued until he became a politician. Until he encountered Herod (government), he had no problems. He begged for nothing, he needed nobody's sympathy.

Whether he was praising or rebuking Herod is not the point . . . he had no business with Herod. Those times were not like now, where you go on television and radio, or use print media, so that the government hears you. For you to say a word that will affect Herod you must become political and have a romance with the government; He started speaking for Phillip, the erstwhile husband of Herodias. That was the downfall of John the Baptist.

There is no one with this Calling which John had, who can survive in a Political setting, because it will remove your cloak as a witness, unfortunately creating a partisan spirit which must be avoided.

No man that warreth entangles himself with the affairs (politics) this world.

Christians can go into politics, in fact they should. Because a man can not cause much changes from the outside. I am not against Christian politicians . . . however those called with the mandate to cry at midnight that the bridegroom cometh CANNOT have anything to do in politics. Politics on this sense goes beyond campaign and voting . . . its witchcraft and manipulation. So the Johns cannot go into politics . . . they must stay in the wilderness and prepare the saints for the work of the Lord and for His coming. Their ministry is not in Herod's palace. They have no business on Herod's table lest they *defile themselves with portion of the king's meat and wine which the king drank* . . . Daniel 1:8.

CHAPTER SEVEN

UNDERSTANDING THE POLITICAL TERRAIN

Some people are prayerfully waiting for a clean political terrain. It cannot be, at least not now. Satan is still the god of this world . . . he still has the legal right to distribute powers to whomsoever he wills . . . How could he have offered Jesus the kingdom of this world and the glory therein, if they were not his? Whatever the believer is or has on earth today in terms of material wealth, is a result of God's grace and his faith in Christ Jesus. That grace however, has not sent Satan to hell yet; which still give him the place as the god of this world. Our exemption from satanic influence is owed to our willingly receiving Jesus into our hearts which brought God kingdom into our hearts. This action, ceased satanic influence over our lives because we have come under the influence of another Lord; to this end, the believer must live by the faith of the finished work of Christ Jesus, being mindful that Satan still controls the affairs of this earth.

John became a politician; the voice has lost its sound. The voice was to 'cry in the wilderness . . . ' when it came to town, it lost its sound. It was no longer a voice but a noise.

No man, with a Calling of heralding the coming of Christ can be a politician, no matter how subtle he enters; he will end up in Herod's prison.

7:1 FLIRTING WITH PHILIP

Philip the former husband of Herodias was also in charge of a Province as Herod was. Both were seasoned politicians. They understood the game and didn't mind trading wives. It was into a scenario like this that John the Baptist came.

Totally neglecting his purpose and mission, John allowed ambition to drag him into Herod's presence. He wanted the government to feel his impact, so he became a voice to Philip. He was supposed to be a voice for God, crying in the wilderness, preparing the world for His coming (Mark 1: 2 TLB). He had heaven's backing as long as he did that, the world came to him in the wilderness, making their way there, struggling to have a glimpse of this Voice that has nothing to do with the palace. (Matthew 11:7:8) Herod respected and feared him, because he was the voice of God . . . then John started speaking or campaigning for Philip, (Matthew 14: 3-4). At that point John became political.

A messenger of God in terms of ministry cannot have a romance with politics. Other children of God may, but not the ones called to 'equip the saints', preparing them for His return. 'Equipping the Saints' and crying in the wilderness are one and the same. For God Calls no man for any other reason.

Many ministers are no longer a voice for God but a voice for Philip. A man becomes a voice for Phillip when he gets Political. A man of God can speak against a failing government; however, it must be from the wilderness. John called them vipers; he told them the axe is laid to the root of the tree. Threatening their very existence yet they feared him. He was the voice of God . . . when men heard God's voice in Mount Heron, they couldn't stand. He has not changed, when we remain His voice, whether we are crying in the wilderness, shouting from the rooftop or at midnight, the impact is the same. It draws men to God and creates reverent fear for Him through us. But when we unfortunately become political, we lose that grace; all we retain is forms of godliness without power.

It will shock you to note how many men of God have become partisan, they are either speaking for Philip or for Herod. 'instead of remaining a spiritual father, giving fair counsel to leadership, they become partisan, though still receiving the applause and honour of men, they have drifted into the prison of Herod.

CHAPTER EIGHT

THE MODERN DAY CULT CALLED GOVERNMENT

Satan hates John the Baptist with passion. Satan's problem is not Jesus but John. Because it's John that would make people believe in Jesus. Satan will do anything to imprison or kill John the Baptist. John is the target. And since John cannot be destroyed because of his location and mission, Satan would try to introduce the word vision to him. This was designed to show him profit and governmental or state relevance. Mission does not look for profit but seeks to please him that called you. Satan deceived John into speaking to Herod, seeing himself as the spiritual adviser to the governor.

Satan is in charge of this world and he has nothing good anyway. When John got political, he (whether he knew or not) got under satanic influence.

Most governments on earth today are run and ruled by cults. The fact that secret cults are at the helm of national affairs is not hidden all over the world. The worry is that John the Baptist is now in Herod's custody.

During the dark Ages and the Crusade, the Emperor Constantine succeeded in marrying the Church and the State. This in turn made Christianity a legal religion and brought it into vogue. This idea, however, brought into Christianity much old pagan worship. These were inculcated into the church's worship and have over the years worsened.

The original idea of Satan is that this "Romance' between the Church and State will be the perfect tool to bring John the Baptist from the wilderness. Thus the relevance of preachers now is connected to how many presidents, governors and other government folks he relates with.

8:1 MODERN HERODS

Satan is still the god of this world and still controls the large portions of earthly governance. Because of this, the devil is very involved in the direct governance of most nations. Understanding Satan's hierarchy is of utmost importance in understanding the power source of most present day leaders. For as much as 'power belongs to our God', He has however, permitted Satan to use authority for a season which shall however soon be taken from him. Satan is making sure he achieves his best before his time expires. Satan has no greater worries than John the Baptist stopped or killed.

By John the Baptist however, I do not refer to the physical one, but his types, who are the genuine Men of God, that must prepare the way for the Lord Jesus Christ' second coming and perfect the saints for work of the ministry.

Satan's most important strategy therefore is to drag John from the wilderness to the palace. This is not physical neither is it measured by material acquisition, but state of mind.

CHAPTER NINE

SATANIC HIERARCHY

Satan's hierarchy is generally made up of four major groups as enumerated in Ephesians 6. There could be others but we are made aware of these in Ephesians 6:12 Paul states that *". . . we wrestle not against flesh and blood, but against principalities, against power, against the rulers of the darkness of this world against spiritual wickedness in high places . . . "*

For want of space and to avoid mis-direction of spiritual energy, we shall not dwell on the jobs of these demonic entities but just brush pass them for the purpose of this treatise.

Principalities are the highest, next to Satan in his kingdom and unlike many thinks, they are not too many. They are the spirits that have direct control over continents. Some might also have control over some other planets and galactic structures. Some are waiting for their leader Satan, to release orders to them so that from other planets, they could invade the earth as Aliens. Principalities take direct orders from Satan and also dispense the same on his behalf. These Principalities have task of demonizing continents and enforcing satanic purposes on continental bases. Like poverty in African, immorality in Europe etc.

Powers, however, deals directly with nations. This is the class of satanic force that distributes leadership authorities in nations. When people join cults or do rituals for political office or seat of authority, they are actually appealing for the approval Powers. The Powers relates to Satan directly having the mandate of demonizing government all over the world. And since men, would not pay the godly price to receive leadership and powers from God, they turn to Satan, who through Principalities and especially, Powers, give them their desired position after the prescribed ritual.

This account for reasons why most governments the world over are laced with cult activities in highly places. The rate, by which occult practices and satanic rituals are rampant in governmental settings, is because the source always sustains the substance. If Satan gives a seat or position through rituals, he will be needing more rituals to sustain it.

This is why a clean political terrain is not in sight for now, until the Lord will raise people who will pay the price for godly power. Power is not free, there is a price. So whether it's coming from God or Satan, it has to be paid for. The power source governs the influence. If it source is from God, it will precipitate good. It is from Satan (as most cases are) it will precipitate evil. No matter how good a person is, if he gets political power through cultic activities, his government must be demonically influenced. For how can you expect a man that killed and sacrificed human blood in order to get a political seat, to do well in governance? His goodwill and fine nature is automatically compromised and influenced by the spirit that gave him the seat . . . he can therefore never lead well.

To get clear picture of satanic operations, you can read my book—BEYOND THE NATURAL.

Satanic activities has however spanned across the frontline of political governance. It has entered into the church, thus Herod is not just clad in military or political attire, and Herod is wearing Bishop Collars and carrying a Bible.

The seduction is so great that John the Baptist is finding it difficult to differentiate King Herod from church leadership.

The romance between the church and the state has left the true John the Baptist confused. Church leadership is now sourcing powers from the same source as political office holders. Satan has taken a hold in high places that those that should rebuke him are dining with him.

I met a man that told me has no respect for pastors because some notable names in the clergy are in the same fraternity with him. That he uses 'his power' for political 'climbing', while they (the pastors) are using theirs to grow their churches. He also revealed that the members of their fraternity will give or 'sow' more into such a pastor's ministry or church to provoke non-members to jealousy. They reasoned that, when those pastors' friends' see that they are having presidents, governors, great political leaders as friends and as people they could invite to their churches and meeting, their friends will begin to envy them. Sooner or later they might woo some John the Baptist into Herod's territory.

David said *'fret not thyself because of evil doers, neither be thou envious against the workers of iniquity for they shall soon be cut down . . . Psalms 37:1-2*

Satan's major target is John the Baptist. Those mandated to baptize the crowd for the coming of the Master. Those appointed to make ready the world for His Second Coming—those whose mission is to equip the saints for the work of the ministry.

As afore mentioned, Satan is not worried about Jesus, he's worried about John, because its John that will make people believes Jesus. Its John's testimony that will validate the claims of Jesus Christ, So Satan target is always John.

CHAPTER TEN

SATAN'S MIGHTEST WEAPON

'. . . again, the devil taketh him up into an exceeding high mountain and sheweth him all the KINGDOMS of the world and the GLORY of them;
And saith unto him, "All these things will I give thee, if thou fall down and worship me . . . " Mathew 4:8-9 KJV

Satan's greatest weapon in his armory is not a bomb, guns, all the likes. Satan's greatest weapon is surprising not in threats of scandals, to take your life or kill you. Killing John in the wilderness is practically impossible to Satan and he knew no amount of bullets unleashed can do John anything as long as he was in the wilderness, heralding the coming of Jesus. Persecutions are a waste of resources against him. The Johns are aware that *". . . they that must live godly in Christ must suffer persecution . . . "* in fact unlike the average modern day believer, the Johns rejoice in persecution, *counting themselves worthy to suffer reproach for the Lord . . .* they don't dodge or compromise to alleviate it.

In these modern times, as long as the truth of the gospel remains in our mouth and we stay in the place of the Calling; satanic on-slaughter is a wasted attempted on us.

Satan knows that man's desire for material acquisition is high. He also knows the effect of the spirit of competition he had sent into the church. Satan understands that our definition of success has been greatly corrupted. All things in the mind gears towards materials; the spiritual has been faked and replaced by staged miracles and staged prophecies.

God's plan, however, is to maintain John in His wilderness position with the spirit of contentment . . . . John must always realize that *'**godliness with contentment is great gain'** 1st Timothy 6:6 (NIV)*. John will not be poor, but he must trust God for his provisions. He can't forge a revelation, he knows that revelations are not conceived but received . . . he is not permitted to stage a miracle to grow his ministry—his food must remain 'locust and wild honey'. Locust and wild honey speaks of trusting God for provision.

It is not a literal locust and wild honey. That analogy brings to life the fact that 'neither John nor any man 'creates locust or wild honey'. The idea is to transfer our dependence on God. He alone creates locust and wild honey and that was all John needed to live. John must be clothed with animal skin. The type God made for Adam when he sinned (Genesis 3:21). John must stay under the covering of Salvation. He's a priest and king unto God, but He must not go into the Palace of Herod. He must reign from the wilderness. Many Herods wear collars now. Many Bishops, Apostles, Prophets are manifested Herods whose destruction is imminent.

Surprisingly, Satan's most dangerous weapon is an offer. An offer for fame, greatness, wealth etc. Who does not like fame, greatness, wealth and power? Who likes to suffer?

The answer to that question is what separates Herod from John. Many John are in Herod's prison, waiting for beheading or gradually transforming to Herod himself.

One scripture that Satan has successfully hidden from most believers is a statement from the very mouth of Jesus Christ recorded in Luke 12:15, it says *"**Take heed and beware of covetousness: for a man's life consisteth not in the abundance of things which he possesseth . . . '**

Satan has appealed to man's mind, re-defining ministry's success as consisting in the abundance of (members, money, materials etc) things which a man possess.

Satan's offer for wealth, fame and the likes is his greatest weapon. It's a short cut designed to bring John to Herod's palace, but the average mind don't see it that way.

Preparing the way for Jesus' coming has nothing to do with Herod. Herod will come to the wilderness if He must be ministered to. Satan is however afraid of the 'few' that refused to fall asleep with the virgins. These are they who must herald the arrival of the bridegroom. Satan must therefore find a way to woo them from the wilderness or lull them to sleep.

Persecution, sandal, assassinations are not Satan's highest weapon. His offer for wealth, fame etc is his highest weapon. That was Satan's last temptation to Jesus Christ. He brought that last because it was his deadliest weapon. The Church is full of fakes, whose romance with the government is physical manifestation of their spiritual ties. They will frustrate any TRUE JOHN who desires a space to bring in sanity into the system. Like a delusion policeman, they will report the informant to the criminal, stating if you don't kill that man, he will continue to report you to the police.

The heart of the true John the Baptist is laced with pain, occasionally doubting their God, wondering why the wicked and fakes are prospering? Why cultist are controlling large crowds in the name of Christianity. The parade of wealth, affluence and influence has practically confused many as it lures more unsuspecting Johns into the dark corridors of powers. This has been Satan final step in every generation. Though it's more pronounced in this generation, David, a true 'fore-runner' of the Messiah

had similar experience. He said, '**But as for me, my feet were almost gone; my steps had well nigh slipped.**
For I was envious at the foolish, when I saw the prosperity of the wicked.
For there are no bands in their death; but their strength is firm. They are not in trouble as other men; neither are they plagued like other men. Therefore, pride compasseth them abut as a chain; violence covereth them as a garment. Their eyes stand out with fitness; they have more than heart could wish. They are corrupt and speak wickedly concerning oppression, they speak lofty, they set their mouth against the heavens, and their tongue walketh through the earth.

"Behold, these are the ungodly, who prosper in the world; they increase in riches.
Verily I have cleansed my heart in vain and washed my hands in innocence.
For all day long, I have been plagued, and chastened every morning.

If I say, I will speak thus; behold I should offend against the generations of thy children.
When I thought to know this, it was too painful for me until I went into the sanctuary of God, then understood I their end.
Surely thou didst set them in slippery places thou castest them down into destruction.

How they are brought into desolation as in a moment they are utterly consumed with terrors. Ps 73:12-19

When David saw the manifestation of those who had become an aberration yet prospering, he almost decided to be like them. The height of compromise in this generation is so heart-rending that it has created confusion in the heart of the true John the Baptist. Herod as of old was totally separated from the church, but this generation has witnessed that Herod is INSIDE the church. Our enemy is wearing our uniform. Creating a picture that John the Baptist will be perceived as a rebel if he chose to remain in the wilderness. Many Johns will refuse to attend many so-called Christian Bodies, and will be viewed as rebels. However the Spirit of God is determined to keep them in the wilderness against all odds.

Many and many more are seeing the prosperity of the wicked, they are seeing the amount of crowd, cash and influence being controlled by those that followed Herod, and they hear the applause and the encomium showered on falsehood. Some heart melts helplessly, while other glides unconsciously or otherwise into Herod's palace to taste of the King's dainty meat. Satan's offer of wealth and fame has received much patronage but the true John is still watching from the wilderness.

In the book of Revelation, God's intention to bring back two notable Old Testament figures was made clear, viz

Elijah and Enoch. God had to bring back Elijah because when he became first, he ended in the wrong place (Herod's Palace Prison). That spirit has being released again and Herod is working on the assassination again. But the confusion in Satan's Kingdom is worse and knows no bound, because with his entire offer, there are some that are saying *"your money perish with you".* They are deliberately *"refusing to fall asleep"* that they may give the midnight cry. Their purposes are so clear that they don't want to trade it for anything. Their mind is made up; we must prepare the way for His second coming, we must cry in the wilderness and we must "perfect the saints" . . . and we must wake up the Bride.

As for those who have accepted Satan's offer, some of them have realized that though they have the fame, wealth and "whatever", they still lack PEACE. They have realized bitterly that what they thought they needed was really not what they needed. But they are already in Herod's Palace. From outside, they desired it, they badly wanted to go in, but once inside, they unfortunately realized it was a prison. Feeling trapped, they are consciously scouting for those to share their woes. By displaying the wares, wears and wealth of Herod's Palace, they woo unsuspecting John's to their already defined doom. When you stumble into these classes of preachers, they are very quick to tell you and show you all their material and physical acquisitions, promptly forgetting that a man's life does not consist of the abundance of things that he possesses.

They can however not help but display such, for that's all they have.

It will amaze you how these ones preach against sin. When you listen to some of these ones preach against sin, it will immediately throw your heart into confusion, because it creates a smoke screen. Supposingly creating a form of righteousness displayed in letters, they mask their true identity.

For even when John was in prison, he still had followers, he still had influence but he had no more power. For how can a man who came in the spirit of Elijah, die in the prison of Herod? On a normal setting, all he needed to do was to call fire, or decree a thing . . . and watch heaven spring into action . . . but he couldn't because he had left his place of power. The power of Elijah was in the wilderness and mountain tops. He must bring the people back to God, so Elijah avoided the palace. As long as John did the same, he was ok until he got into Herod's custody.

In vs. 13 of Psalms 73, David said at some point, he thought that his staying with God's purpose was a waste, he felt his continuing as God's voice in the wilderness was not worth it, when he saw cultist as pastors of large congregation and falsehood celebrated and applauded, the man almost backslide. He said, *"I have cleansed my heart in vain"* because he saw iniquity in the high places, but when he returned to the place of his Calling, he saw that beyond their material acquisition and public applauds, this erstwhile John are already in Herod's custody waiting the gallows. In David's own words, he said ***"I went into the sanctuary (the place of Calling), then understood I their end" Psalms 73:7***

CHAPTER ELEVEN

HERODIAS THE MOTHER OF COMPROMISE

Historically, Herodias was the daughter of Aristobulus, son of Herod the Great. Aristobulus mother was Marianne, daughter of Hyrcanus. Herodias second husband was Herod Antipas, he was tetrarch of Galilee and Peraea (3-39AD), he was the son of the same Herod the Great, but his mother was Malthace.

Herod Antipas was therefore a step brother of Aristobulus, the father of Herodias. Some historical controversy abound regarding the identity of her first husband for who she had the daughter that danced in Matthew 14: 3, Mark 6:17 and Luke 3:19. He was called Philip the brother of Herod Antipas, that name however was missing in Josephus account and other ancient manuscripts. Josephus account records he was Herod, also son of Herod the Great, but his mother was named Marianne who was a daughter of Simon the high priest—this puts him as step brother of Herod Antipas (Josephus, Ant, XVIII, V, and IV).

According to the above historical accounts, Herodias flirted between two brothers. In fact you could almost call it incest because she was related to both. Herodias speaks of a seductive power whose main pre-occupation is to create a partisan-setting for John. Her desire for power like Jezebel in such that she must connect herself to the highest form of authority, for only then can her impact be felt. Reading the account of Josephus further, one would immediately see how her ambition proved the ruin of Herod Antipas. Herodias, being Jealous of the authority that Agrippa her brother wielded, induced Herod to demand the Caligula, which was the official title of the king. However, Agrippa through machinations refused, and Herod was banished.

Herodias was actually the one that demanded for the head of John. Since she was his subject or topic, and since John made her his target message, she decided to plot her graph against him. She therefore used the forces at her disposal (her head and her offspring) to get John killed. Her head, of-course speaks of her husband while her offspring speaks of her daughter. Herodias might not represent a person in our generation but she speaks about cultism. John said it was wrong for leaders to be involved in cultism. Was he correct? Yes, But he should released his bullets from the wilderness.

Herodias wants John dead. She must however pass through Herod and her daughter to do it.

Herod and his palace are the wealth, fame etc that Satan has to offer, Herodias is the brain behind it.

The romance or marriage between the church and cultism in the name of large crowd, beautiful cars, magnificent building and the workings of miracles are all the seductive work of Herodias. Her inability to get John on her side is what endangers John's life.

Very many that started well in the faith, but has unfortunately come under the influence of Herodias. Seeing their friends and colleagues in nice cars, controlling great crowds and wielding authority and fame, many have strayed or contemplated the idea of siding Herodias.

I met a young man, who had most things money could buy and has a large following in his congregation. He told me that it was a notable "man of God" that changed his life. On further enquiries he revealed how he was taught to bury things in his church and collect sand from various places for the "exercise or ritual". Amazingly this young man doesn't see anything wrong in what he has done, apparently because of his desire for wealth and fame, and also his regard for the "man of God" that showed him. You can only wonder how many people are serving God now.

Herodias, who is fronting for Satan, is seducing the people of God so fast that the deception of this generation has superseded that of all history. Falsehood was easily discernable in those days, because you could see things that spelt falsehood. If you walk into a church, that is using colored candles etc . . . for instance, it creates a check in your spirit. But now the deception is so polished that it could pass as truth. Jesus said it all targeted at deceiving the elect. Falsehood has been refined and it dances with us daily, it has learnt our dance-step, so we can't differentiate it anymore . . . Herodias has mastered the act of seduction in and it spells doom for John the Baptist. The populaces are confused because they don't know what to believe. Even major national Christian bodies have accepted and celebrate falsehood. Young believers don't know where to follow. The sound of the music to which Herodias daughter is dancing, is deafening the ears of the average believers, making it almost impossible to hear the voice of the Spirit of God. Our confidence is however anchored on the fact *'that the triumphing of the wicked is short and the joy of the hypocrite but for a moment? Though his Excellency mounts up to the heavens, and his head reach unto the clouds; yet he shall perish forever like his own dung; they which have seen him shall say; where is he?' Job 20:5-9*

CHAPTER TWELVE

THE DANCE

Woe to them that goeth down to Egypt for help . . . Isaiah 31:1.

A dance is a rhythmic movement of the body. It is often in response to a music tune. Whether audible or not, music can make people dance. In the same vein, types of music determine types of dance. Just as we have Rock, Disco, Makossa etc, which determines types of dance-steps, there are satanic rhythm to which a lot of people are dancing.

When you see people act in certain ways, or better still, the way some people act is determined by the music that their spirit is dancing to. Satan can compel people to dance to his desired music. He could use pressure from friends and family to cause people to dance to his tune. But a person can't hear Satan's drumming except he's first disconnected from the heavenly vibes.

When Jesus gave the parable of the sower in the gospel of Matthew in the thirteenth chapter, he indicated that the seed fell into four categories of grounds . . . way side, stony place, thorns and Good soil. Studying the passage reveals that the seed didn't grow at all in two categories of soil . . . that is *'way side'* and those *'among thorns'*. The ones by the wayside didn't grow because TIME was not given to them. The birds of the air came IMMEDIATELY and took them. That suggests that if they had enough time, they might have grown. We have seen seeds cracking through tarred pavements and germinating by sidewalks. Seeds can grow even by the wayside, given enough time. The seed however among THORNS didn't grow; its problem wasn't time, its problem was that the seed in the 'WRONG COMPANY'. It was among thorns. Bible said *' . . . the THORNS sprang up and choked them . . . '* Matthew 13:7. Later, as the Lord expanded the parable; He said the *"THORNS are the cares of this world and the deceitfulness of riches . . . "* Matthew 13:22

As seen in the chapter before, Satan's mightiest weapon is not a bullet, neither is it any kind of affliction. His greatest force and weapon is in his offer of wealth, fame and fortune as he proposed to the Lord Jesus Christ.

The desire for wealth is so great that is STOPPED the natural process of the seed. The seed would naturally grow or at least make attempt to. But the ones that fell among thorns never grow. The thorns grew instead.

Many Christians and ministers have succumbed to the music that is being orchestrated by Satan; they have crowded themselves with the wrong folks. All their emphasis in life is within the perimeter of wealth, fame and fortune. This compromise, deceit, cultism has danced its way into the church and because so called fathers in the Lord promote this music and its dancers from their exalted pulpit, it has thereby legalized and rubber-stamped falsehood.

A pastor's success is therefore measured by his congregational strength or size, his material acquisition and the authority he wields in Christendom. To this end, falsehood has thrived as it consciously choked the seed of GOD'S TRUTH.

I am a Blessed man. God's church in my care (Champion Faith Assembly) is growing daily and we are expanding daily into countries we never thought we could reach. I am also very financially comfortable. I have said those to establish the fact that I am not against wealth or comfort. I am under a Divine Mandate to make us see how our camp has being infiltrated. While we lift our hands to worship God and dance to the chorus in the church house, our hearts are practically dancing to another tune. Some few years ago, I was with a friend in Baltimore, Maryland in the United States when he got an email. The email apparently was not meant for him. I am sure the sender took him for someone else. When my friend showed me the email, tears filled my eyes.

It was from a very notable and popular Bishop, who has visited many African countries and other parts of the world 'preaching the gospel'. My friends had sent a previous email to him, based on their discussion about their vision for soul-winning. They had met in an international conference of Bishops, where they exchanged contacts.... in response to my friends email, this Bishop said '... *you sound like you are one of those serious people in this church thing, like I told you earlier, I am not a Christian. I realized early in life that these preachers wield a lot of power and wealth, so I purpose in my heart to learn the act. For these years, I have done well, grown and gained a lot of grounds and respects. I am planning to retire soon, after milking these* **'fishes'**, *I'll go to the Caribbean, get myself some hot babes and drink* ...* '* these are a part of that email. I also paraphrased some. I told my friend to send it to a Bishop in Nigeria or to another Bishop in the country where we received the email and he rightly said, 'how do you know if it was not meant for the person you want to tell'?

A bishop, notable one; He said "I AM NOT A CHRISTIAN" yet he preaches every Sunday, travelling all over the world, fooling who?

Wealth will go to those who have sold their soul to the devil. Satan doesn't care whether they carry the bible; he doesn't care whether they say Jesus is Lord. That's not his problem; he has successfully used them to create a counterfeit church to confuse the populace. He knows they are already his and they dance to his tune . . . their destiny is sealed. The bible says a curse is hanging on those who have gone to Egypt for help. The righteous are confused and almost disheartened at the prosperity of the wicked. They increase in their cultic practices and God seem to be quiet and comfortable with it. The wisest man that ever lived, who is described as 'The Preacher" said in Ecclesiastes 8:11 *". . . because sentence against an evil work is not executed speedily, therefore the heart of the sons of men is FULLY SET in them to do evil".*

Many are being lured into the dance. They see evil prospering and there's no SUDDEN judgment, they concluded that it's vain to be righteous. The dance of Herodias daughter was not originally designed to kill John. She was just dancing. But Herodias, wanted John dead and the perfect way was to use the dance.

The dance of Herodias daughter was design for immediate gratification as is always the case. Satan can give you anything that satisfies the immediate but he always has a long term plan. Herodias' desire to see John dead was such a passion that she must have taken time to plan it and waited patiently for its opportunity.

Anytime you see folks in the scripture go after immediate wealth, they forfeit their future. There are many ministers of the gospel now who seem to wield so much authority and wealth who will not have successors from their loins because the death of John the Baptist terminates the linage of Zechariah—pronounced 'Zekaryah' in the Hebrew, it mean 'Jah remembers'. The idea of the devil is to totally remove the remembrance of God from the earth. And since John the Baptist is the custodian of the oracle of God, he must be killed. However, Satan has successfully blended some church leaders with the state on a demonic blenders, the remaining idea of Satan is to heighten his music so that even the very elect might start dancing.

Without the dance, John can't be killed. It has to be seductive enough. It has to be appealing enough. The trend is horrifying. The rate at which the younger generation of gospel ministers crave "success" and the alarming rate at which they are being recruited by already contaminated "fathers" are nothing short of direct invitations into Herod's prison . . . to which some have ignorantly danced into.

Herod wanted John dead, but as long as John was in the wilderness, even king Herod feared him. His death will cause the kind of riot that Herod wasn't prepared for. Herod wanted to kill John, but he was afraid . . . Matthew 14:5 (NIV). The man was feared even by the king. God designed it so. As long as we are in the wilderness, and are awake at the midnight and give the cry from the mountain top, we are feared, even by the leaderships of the cults and states. John' ministry was so clear to all that in *Mark 11:32*, even unbelievers couldn't say he was an ordinary man.

Satan's appeal to the mind of John is to offer him what every mind wants. Because the heart cannot delight in what the mind rejects. So the mind has to be appealed to. For as earlier said, the mind is the seat of vision and ambition, which had become John's problems.

The word of God, which John was in custody of, is the only tool that separates the mind and the spirit (Hebrew 4:12), but when John found his way into Herod's prison, he lost touch with God's word and his mind became more active than his spirit. This in turn makes materials more appealing than spirituals. John manifested the quality of one who had lost it. Three things characterizes a man that has entered Herod's prison.

He first develops a high spirit of competition, feeling so insecure by the progress of others. John was offended by the progress of Jesus. While he was in the wilderness, he even told his disciples to follow Jesus. He didn't mind them not returning back to him. He said the best man rejoices for the groom. But when he got into the prison all that changed. He got competitive.

Secondly, he got very materialistic. Competition is usually measured by physical acquisitions. The size of the congregation, the car you drive and other material possessions. Like afore measured, when you ever meet these classes of folks, all they throw at you is their material gains.

Thirdly they change their previous confessions. In the name of new revelation, they justify their actions at the detriment of their spiritual life. It was the same John that said *"he must increase while I decrease"* . . . he said *"behold the lamb of God".* When he was in prison and the disciples came to him, John sent messages to Jesus *"are you the Christ or we should look for another"?*

John changed his confession because he had become dull spiritually. These are those that, like the prodigal son who was miles away from the Father's presence, started feeding swine. The very thing they forbid to touch years ago (as the Jews forbid to touch pigs), the very they spoke against years ago, they now confidently support it, justifying their love for materialism . . . when you see such, know you are staring at a man in the prison of Herod.

I am not against wealth, as I am a very blessed man. The emphasis however is that the compromise and the loss of the Voice is a result of the seduction to come into Herod's palace.

Most modern day preachers have lost touch with the desire of the Spirit of God. This is unavoidably so, because a man cannot be material minded and still hear the whispers of the Spirit. We must not confuse the manifestation of prophecies, healing and miracles to the move of the Holy Spirit. Neither must be think those are the genuine seal of the Holy Spirit on a man's Calling or Ministry. These seeming working of miracles (some of which are staged) can actually be made possible by Satan. How can we be surprised that Satan can work miracles, when the Bible is clear about that—The spiritual insensitivity of the church is so baffling that the fact about 'lying wonders' as recorded in 2nd Thess. 2:9 is overlooked.

I believe in miracles, I have seen and still do see miracles of all shapes and sizes. I am also aware that God is still working miracles, and like Rev. Yinka Yusuf will say 'miracles are forever' and I believe it.

However, many unsuspecting men and women of God are lured into friendship or sonship with many so-called 'fathers' whose deep relationship with occult is so covered and smoke screened that the 'young John the Baptist' sees it as a privilege or open door to be associated with such big names. Seeing it as a privilege and opportunity, has therefore closed the ears of these young men of God. Desiring to have the kind of crowd, fame and fortune of these big names, these young John's have unfortunately wondered into the premises of Herod, seeing it as open door.

Not many relate with God or His Spirit anymore, but rather with these men, whose romance with cult and government has legalized politics and falsehood in the church, magnifying physical prosperity against spiritual well being. They will do the bidding of the fathers while directly shunning the inner witness and Voice of the Spirit. The hitherto sensitive brother has thrown away his spiritual alertness in exchange for "open door" with the "great platform".

That a man distributed rice and clothes, (we do that too in our ministry) does not make him a man of God or approved of God, because even the atheist does that. The scripture says it's possible to bestow all one's goods to the poor . . . and still not get God's approval *1st Cor. 13:3*.

But those acts, because of the material nature of man, have become the yardstick of measuring a person's ingenuity especially when it is laced with some forms of miracles.

A man was confessing recently, how part of their occult rituals is to give out gifts of food and clothes to the poor. These, however increases their occult strength because most people who receives those gifts, later dies from incurable disease. Off-course no one hears about that. Video and televise the acts of giving out to confuse the populace and buy credibility, and its working because these acts has idolized falsehood.

This has greatly hurt God's heart as His people can hardly have time with Him and for Him. The Truth is suffering, being choked by the thorns of the deceitfulness of riches.

I hear of a man of God who spoke of swallowing a frog in order to perform miracles, prophecy accurately and grow a large. The young men are confused about needing an extra help other than the Holy Spirit to do God's work for God. They are bothered about why something must be dug in God's house to help God's work grow . . .

Let's see this *"I saw three unclean spirit like frogs come out of the mouth of the dragon and out of the mouth of the beast, and out of the mouth of the false prophet."*

For they are the spirit of devils, WORKING MIRACLES, which go forth unto the kings . . . Rev. 16:13-14

The genuine John the Baptist does not see a connection to a president, governor or any physical ruler as a breakthrough or open door. The physical or government official should actually lobby to meet the man of God as they did with Jesus. However because of the occultic romance or marriage between the "leaders" of the church and the politicians of the state, the mundane has gained the spiritual seat of prominence, thereby un-sitting ingenuity.

Judging success by the physical acquisition or the fame that is wielded by anyone is the obvious measuring rod for the church's spiritual state.

As Elijah fled from Jezebel in 1 kings 19, God took the time to teach Elijah a strong lesson that we can't overlook. Elijah left town and headed for the wilderness. He went for three reasons, First of all, was the fear for his life. Jezebel would kill him just as Herodias would demand for John's head. Many theologians have wondered why Elijah should run from Jezebel when he had just killed the prophets of Baal. Elijah knew that if he is not located in the place of his strength, Jezebel could kill him, regardless of his previous victories over Baal. Herodias and Jezebel can only be handled from the wilderness setting. That's the place of our strength. God can only protect John (Elijah) in the wilderness. That's where his protection and provision are. John ate locust and wild honey. Both delicacies were not manmade, God was inferring that He will personally provide and care for His servants.

As seen in 1 Kings 19, from vs. 4, Elijah had to wisely retreat to the wilderness. Though frustrated and wishing for death and seeing himself as a failure, the Lord immediately resumed His commitment of provision and security because Elijah had come 'Home". He had returned from the palace and was lucky not to have died or imprisoned before the self-realization.

On arrival, the angel woke him out of his frustration and gave him food. He could only eat the food of God because he came back to the wilderness. The palace is a trap for John the Baptist. The fame and fortune paraded by those in Herod palace is their doom, for their soul has been exchanged for such.

God's commitment is still to those in the wilderness. Even after Elijah ate, he was still sleepy, for his stay in the city had sedated his spirit. God had to feed him again to strengthen him enough for the journey. God had to teach him something that will benefit him when he returns as John the Voice and the fore-runner. Unfortunately he didn't learn, but since these things are written *"for our examples and admonition, upon whom the ends of the world are come" (1st Cor. 10:11)*, it's of utmost importance that we understand them.

From vs. 11 of 1st Kings 19, God began the great lesson, **'And he said, Go forth, and stand upon the mount before the Lord, And behold, the LORD passed by and a great and strong wind rent the mountains, and broke in pieces the rocks before the LORD, but the LORD WAS NOT in the wind: and after the wind an earthquake, but the LORD WAS NOT in the earthquake. And after the earthquake a fire, but the LORD WAS NOT in the fire: and after the fire A STILL SMALL VOICE"**

The above passage reveals three strong physical phenomenons which cannot be ignored or overlooked. They represent the four elements of nature . . . The wind, earthquakes, water and the fire. The bible says the Wind tore rocks and moved mountains. It made cripples to walk. Blind eyes saw, miracles happened. BUT THE LORD WAS NOT IN THE WIND. After the wind, an Earthquake. It had national effect, it was heard of everywhere. The news media blew it and it was noised abroad. It was like CNN and BBC announcing an earthquake that happened somewhere. The earthquake attracts international audience BUT THE LORD WAS NOT IN THE EARTHQUAKE . . . hmmm this is worth thinking about! God doesn't necessarily approve what we applaud.

After the earthquake a FIRE! I heard of a cult whose emblem is 'fire' the fire speaks to its members, enabling them to perform miracles and grow their church. For those members who are not pastors, the cult grants them 'success' in their chosen field as long as they comply with certain rules. Fire is a universal currency with the same effect everywhere. It's attractive, yet judgmental and can't be overlooked. That someone was judged because he spoke about a *'man of God'* doesn't immediately approve the man of God. Because Satan will do anything to protect his own also. Including destroying opposition to those he had anointed to lead many astray—THE LORD WAS NOT IN THE FIRE.

It's amazing how and where we see the LORD. For while we 'think' we are seeing the Lord, in the crowd, miracles, fame and wealth displayed by some folks, we might actually be looking at Satan himself masquerading as an angel of light. (1 Cor. 11:14) and the scriptures further says 'it is not surprising, then if his servants masquerades as servants of righteousness (11 Cor. 11:15).

As mentioned earlier, I am not against crowd, fame and wealth. I am a custodian of these, but they must however not be the bases of approval neither should they be a yardstick for ministerial success.

The poorest way to see God is to search for Him in WIND, EARTHQUAKES and FIRE. He is not compulsorily there! The scripture says 'after the fire A STILL SMALL VOICE. The voice is still and small. It can only be heard in the serenity of a wilderness. Many no longer hear it. The music of Herod's palace has drowned it. And as true to His nature, the Spirit of God will not strive with man (Gen 6:3), so as you step out of the wilderness, you are deafened to the voice.

You have to know the voice in order to be a voice. John was the voice crying in the wilderness, but he must know the voice of his Master—Jesus said my sheep know my voice; still and gentle voice that what it is.

THE SWAP
There's another strange lesson or incident in the scripture that is begging for attention. In Exodus 32, Moses was on his way down from the mountain with Joshua. Both represented separate generations. For as much as one was notable and wielded great authority, the other was silently learning wisdom. For as much as one grew up in the palace, went to the wilderness and returned to the palace, the other one never had a palace experience at all. They were Moses and Joshua. Educated as master in the

academic strength of his day, Moses was not a figure for play. But since God can't speak to him in the palace, for the sounds of the palace music can't be allowed to mar or distort the still small voice, it became of necessity that he (Moses) be invited to the wilderness. For only in such serenity and setting will he hear the still SMALL VOICE in its uncompromising form. After some years, circumstances took him back to the familiar palace, this time to bring back God's people, but God in His wisdom know that such can't be trusted to take the people into the promise land for those have become accustomed to PHYSICAL phenomenon such as plagues, wind, earthquakes and fire. These will make them to miss Him anytime He speaks and seeks that they obey the voice. It was no wonder that Moses disobeyed the voice and smote the ROCK instead of speaking to it. Moses, by his palace experience has removed the premium from the voice and placed it on some physical manifestation; hence God was offended and could not trust him to bring the people into the land of promise.

But contrary to Moses, was Joshua who was actually brought into the ministry by Moses. He had no romance with the palace. Jesus Christ, in speaking about John, *said what went ye out into the wilderness to see, A reed shaken with the wind? But what went ye out for to see, A man clothed in soft raiment? Behold, they that wear soft clothing are in kings houses . . . "* then he concluded that John was more than a prophet. Joshua by his upbringing was a wilderness man. Who by divine providence was a follower of Moses. However the experience on the Mountain reveals something about the sensitivity of the twain.

In Exodus 32:15 " . . . ***And Moses turned, and went down from the mountain and the two tables of testimony were in his hand: the tables were written on both their sides, on the one side and on the other were they written . . .***
Vs 17 " . . . Ad when Joshua HEARD the noise of the people as they shouted, he said unto Moses, There is a noise of WAR in the camp
Vs 18: 'And he (Moses) said, it is not the voice of them that shout for mastery, neither is it the voice that cries for being overcome: but the noise of them that sing do I hear . . .

Moses, though a father, has his ears accustomed with palace experience which is majorly characterized by singing and dancing: the palace is the last place to hear sound of war. It is mostly a place of celebrations, after-all that was where Herodias daughter performed.

Joshua on the contrary, though a son or under-minister to Moses, had a wilderness void of physical glory. His custom wasn't singing and dancing, He served a God that wants His people to WORSHIP HIM in the WILDERNESS. Exodus 5:1. '***. . . Let My people go, that they may hold a feast unto me in the WILDERNESS.*** To God, it is not so much as the beauty of the place that influences Him. He wants those who are not moved neither are they affected by physical luxury, whose ears are tuned to Him by virtue of their wilderness experience. How then can we wonder when God shows up in Jacob's dream in the middle of NOWHERE, (a clear wilderness) . . . the patriarch wakes up and say *'surely the LORD is in this place; and I knew it not (Genesis 28:16),* where else could God be?

Joshua, because of his disposition, had no choice but to hear into the spirit, having spent so much time in the wilderness and used to the still small voice; he announced to his father-in-the Lord (Moses) that he could hear the sound of war. His father in the Lord patted him at the back and said "boy! They are singing!" Where they singing? YES. That's what the physical ears heard. But Satan had launched war against the new born nation to extinguish them; it was that spiritual battle sound that Joshua heard.

In this same vein, many so called sons are seen and deemed as rebellious because they can't help but hear the sound of war. They see and perceive that the church is being adulterated and polluted. They see how Satan and falsehood has taken a high seat in the church and are being applauded and celebrated. Their ears, fine-tuned by their wilderness experiences, they hear the sound of war. But while the Moses' are celebrating large congregation, staged miracles and false prophecy, the Joshua's are hearing the sound of war.

Though Moses had been used greatly (may be greater than Joshua), it is however against the principle of Divinity that he take the people into the promise land. It was all a problem of hearing. When Moses became confronted by the reality that it was actually WAR disguised in singing, his frustration knew no bounds. He broke the very commandment that God handed to him. His anger took over. The truth is that he broke it, before he got off the mountain. When he said it was a voice of singing, he lost the authority to hold on to the WORD. A man can't be carried away by WIND, 'FIRES AND EARTHQUAKES' and still hear the 'still small voice.

For this course, it became imperative that the baton should shift from Moses to Joshua.

To balance this treaty, it is important to state that, I have not inferred that every large congregation is not of God, neither have I have said every spiritual father is in Herod's prison. We however know that in every generation, the Lord leaves a remnant for Himself.

CHAPTER THIRTEEN

LAST WORDS

As Jesus transfigured before the Apostles, two of the Old Testament major figures stood before him. They were Moses and Elijah. And as this Age winds up, the Two Witnesses referred to in Rev 11, are said to carry tremendous powers. Theologians agree that they are Elijah and Enoch who had not tasted physical death during their earthly sojourn. It is very safe to note that John the Baptist came in the spirit of Elijah. This spirit was needed to herald the coming of Jesus Christ, either His First Coming or Second Coming for no other Call is necessary other than that of John to fore run His coming. The Witnesses are also empowered to pass-judgment as they operate within the confines of their ministry.

If they will not be seduced or allow the unnecessary competition that prevails in the palace to contaminate them, they will wield tremendous power. If they are not drowned by the political flood, they will show forth great power to God's glory.

From the two Witnesses mentioned above, Elijah was a constant. We could however substitute John for Elijah. Whereas Elijah was a success in his ministry; He also had the threats of the palace. What we see as an opportunity, Elijah saw as a trap. Hence he ran back to wilderness, which was his place of strength. Dear man of God, your strength is still in the wilderness not in the palace. Jesus was there, he retreated to that place often. While John was there, the whole town came to him. It was in that setting that Jacob has his dream where he saw angels ascending and descending.

God is not against our prosperity, he wants it and actually delights in it, but it must be "locust, wild honey and camel's hair". These speak of total and absolute dependence on God. Locust, wild honey or camels are not men's products. These are all God's direct products and they speak of the prophet's total leaning on God.

Yes, the temptation of straying abounds with greater intensity every day, yet we must remember that no matter what we posses on earth in terms of materials and fame, God doesn't accredit us with man's yardstick neither is His score-card the same as men.

Every minister of the gospel must therefore see themselves as John the Baptist, with the ministry to the world for the Second Coming of Jesus Christ. We must see ourselves as those giving the midnight cry that the Bridegroom Cometh.

The music is on and Herodias daughter is dancing, Herodias wants John dead but where is John now? in the wilderness or in the Palace cell?